interchange
FOURTH EDITION

Jack C. Richards

With Jonathan Hull and Susan Proctor

Series Editor: David Bohlke

CAMBRIDGE
UNIVERSITY PRESS

WORKBOOK

2A

CAMBRIDGE UNIVERSITY PRESS
Cambridge, New York, Melbourne, Madrid, Cape Town,
Singapore, São Paulo, Delhi, Mexico City

Cambridge University Press
32 Avenue of the Americas, New York, NY 10013-2473, USA

www.cambridge.org
Information on this title: www.cambridge.org/9781107616981

© Cambridge University Press 2013

This publication is in copyright. Subject to statutory exception
and to the provisions of relevant collective licensing agreements,
no reproduction of any part may take place without the written
permission of Cambridge University Press.

First published 1998
Third edition 2005

Printed in Lima, Peru, by Empresa Editora El Comercio S.A.

A catalog record for this publication is available from the British Library.

ISBN 978-1-107-64869-2 Student's Book 2 with Self-study DVD-ROM
ISBN 978-1-107-64410-6 Student's Book 2A with Self-study DVD-ROM
ISBN 978-1-107-62676-8 Student's Book 2B with Self-study DVD-ROM
ISBN 978-1-107-64873-9 Workbook 2
ISBN 978-1-107-61698-1 Workbook 2A
ISBN 978-1-107-65075-6 Workbook 2B
ISBN 978-1-107-62527-3 Teacher's Edition 2 with Assessment Audio CD/CD-ROM
ISBN 978-1-107-62941-7 Class Audio CDs 2
ISBN 978-1-107-62500-6 Full Contact 2 with Self-study DVD-ROM
ISBN 978-1-107-63719-1 Full Contact 2A with Self-study DVD-ROM
ISBN 978-1-107-65092-3 Full Contact 2B with Self-study DVD-ROM

For a full list of components, visit www.cambridge.org/interchange

Cambridge University Press has no responsibility for the persistence or
accuracy of URLs for external or third-party Internet Web sites referred to in
this publication and does not guarantee that any content on such Web sites is,
or will remain, accurate or appropriate. Information regarding prices, travel
timetables, and other factual information given in this work is correct at
the time of first printing but Cambridge University Press does not guarantee
the accuracy of such information thereafter.

Art direction, book design, layout services, and photo research: Integra
Audio production: CityVox, NYC
Video production: Nesson Media Boston, Inc.

Contents

Credits

Illustrations

Andrezzinho: 11; **Daniel Baxter:** 28, 38, 41, 48, 88; **Carlos Diaz:** 6, 77, 94; **Jada Fitch:** 17, 42; **Tim Foley:** 22, 80; **Dylan Gibson:** 86, 92; **Chuck Gonzales:** 4, 34, 67; **Joaquin Gonzalez:** 35, 59; **Dan Hubig:** 90; **Trevor Keen:** 13, 21 (*bottom*), 55, 72, 83 (*top*); **KJA-artists:** 2, 36, 50 (*left and center*), 84, 91; **Greg Lawhun:** 16, 68, 87

Monika Melnychuk: 39 (*right*) **Karen Minot:** 10, 15, 27, 65, 89; **Ortelius Design:** 30 (*map*), 64; **Rob Schuster:** 30, 45, 51, 54, 63, 73, 83 (*bottom center*), 93; **Daniel Vasconcellos:** 19, 31, 71; **James Yamasaki:** 1, 32, 79, 85; **Rose Zgodzinski:** 18, 39 (*left*), 40, 57, 75, 78, 81; **Carol Zuber-Mallison:** 3, 9, 21(*top*), 33, 50 (*top and bottom*), 69, 87

Photos

3 © Allstar Picture Library/Alamy
5 © Denkou Images/Alamy
7 (*top, left to right*) © Glowimages/Getty Images; © Dennis MacDonald/age footstock; (*middle, left to right*) © Stacy Walsh Rosenstock/Alamy; © Bill Freeman/Alamy; (*bottom, left to right*) © Lee Snider/The Image Works; © Richard Lord/PhotoEdit
8 © Michael Dwyer/Alamy
10 (*top, left to right*) © Jane Sweeney/Robert Harding World Imagery/Corbis; © Jon Arnold Images Ltd/Alamy; © VisualHongKong/Alamy; © One-image photography/Alamy
12 © Jason O. Watson/Alamy
14 (*right, top to bottom*) © Exactostock/SuperStock; © Frank van den Bergh/iStockphoto
18 (*top right*) © Alberto Pomares/iStockphoto; (*bottom, left to right*) © Betty Johnson/Dbimages/Alamy; © Mustafa Ozer/AFP/Getty Images
20 © iStockphoto/Thinkstock
23 © Tupporn Sirichoo/iStockphoto
25 © RubberBall/SuperStock
27 (*left, top to bottom*) © Licia Rubinstein/iStockphoto; © Raga Jose Fuste/Prisma Bildagentur AG/Alamy; © Radharcimages.com/Alamy
29 © Yagi Studio/Digital Vision/Getty Images
30 (*top inset*) © iStockphoto/Thinkstock; (*middle*) © Andrey Devyatov/iStockphoto
37 (*left to right*) © i love images/Alamy; © Ricardoazoury/iStockphoto; © Erik Simonsen/Photographer's Choice/Getty Images; © Angelo Arcadi/iStockphoto; © Martyn Goddard/Corbis
43 (*right, top to bottom*) © Daniel Dempster Photography/Alamy; © Tetra Images/Getty Images
46 (*right, top to bottom*) © Glow Asia/Alamy; © David Young-Wolff/PhotoEdit
47 (*left to right*) © Eye Ubiquitous/SuperStock; © Hisham Ibrahim/Photographer's Choice/Getty Images; © Bill Bachmann/Alamy; © Brand X Pictures/Thinkstock

49 © Bettmann/Corbis
52 © Hermann Erber/LOOK Die Bildagentur der Fotografen GmbH/Alamy
54 © Bruno Perousse/age footstock
58 (*top left*) © Vadym Drobot/Shutterstock; (*middle right*) © Juan Carlos Tinjaca/Shutterstock; (*middle left*) © Alena Ozerova/Shutterstock; (*bottom right*) © Stuart Jenner/Shutterstock; (*bottom left*) © iStockphoto/Thinkstock
61 © Florian Kopp/Imagebroker/Alamy
62 (*top, left to right*) © Luciano Mortula/Shutterstock; © Anibal Trejo/Shutterstock; © Julian Love/John Warburton-Lee Photography/Alamy; (*middle, left to right*) © Bill Bachman/Alamy; © Juergen Richter/LOOK Die Bildagentur der Fotografen GmbH/Alamy; © Goran Bogicevic/Shutterstock
63 (*middle, top to bottom*) © Bernardo Galmarini/Alamy; © Ariadne Van Zandbergen/Alamy
64 © Josef Polleross/The Image Works
65 (*top right*) © Robert Landau/Surf/Corbis; (*bottom right*) © Travel Pictures/Alamy
66 © Hulton-Deutsch Collection/Historical/Corbis
69 © Globe Photos/ZUMAPRESS/NEWSCOM
70 © Han Myung-Gu/WireImage/Getty Images
73 © WALT DISNEY PICTURES/Album/NEWSCOM
74 © XPhantom/Shutterstock
75 (*top left*) © Bettmann/Corbis; (*top right*) © Sunset Boulevard/Historical/Corbis
76 © Buyenlarge/Archive Photos/Getty Images
78 © LIONSGATE/Album/NEWSCOM
82 © Mark Gibson/Danita Delimont Photography/NEWSCOM
83 (*all*) © ahmet urkac/Shutterstock
95 © Workbook Stock/Getty Images
96 © maXx images/SuperStock

A time to remember

Past tense

A Write the past tense of these verbs.

Verb	Past tense	Verb	Past tense
be	was / were	hide	_____
become	_____	laugh	_____
do	_____	lose	_____
email	_____	move	_____
get	_____	open	_____
have	_____	scream	_____

B Complete this paragraph. Use the past tense of each of the verbs in part A.

My best friend in school ____was____ Michael.
He and I _____ in Mrs. Gilbert's third-grade
class, and we _____ friends.
We often _____ crazy things in class, but I don't
think Mrs. Gilbert ever really _____ mad at us.
For example, Michael _____ a pet monkey named
Bananas. Sometimes he _____ it in Mrs. Gilbert's
desk. Later, when she _____ the
drawer, she always _____ loudly,
and the class _____ . After two
years, Michael's family _____ to another town.
We _____ each other for a few years, but then
we _____ contact. I often wonder what
he's doing now.

1

2 Complete the questions in this conversation.

Mary: Welcome to the building. My name's Mary Burns.

Sílvio: Hello. I'm Sílvio Mendes. It's nice to meet you.

Mary: Nice to meet you, too. Are you from around here?

Sílvio: No, I'm from Brazil.

Mary: Oh, really? <u>Were you born</u> in Brazil?

Sílvio: No, I wasn't born there, actually. I'm originally from Portugal.

Mary: That's interesting. So, when _____ to Brazil?

Sílvio: I moved to Brazil when I was in elementary school.

Mary: Where _____ ?

Sílvio: We lived in Recife. It's a beautiful city in northeast Brazil. Then I went to college.

Mary: _____ to school in Recife?

Sílvio: No, I went to school in São Paulo.

Mary: And what _____ ?

Sílvio: Oh, I studied engineering. But I'm here to go to graduate school.

Mary: Great! When _____ ?

Sílvio: I arrived last week. I start school in three days.

Mary: Well, good luck. And sorry for all the questions!

3 Answer these questions.

1. Where were you born?

   _____

2. Did your family move when you were a child?

   _____

3. Did you have a favorite teacher in elementary school?

   _____

4. What hobbies did you have when you were a kid?

   _____

5. When did you begin to learn English?

   _____

4 *Rodrigo Santoro*

A Scan the article about Rodrigo Santoro. Where is he from? What does he do?

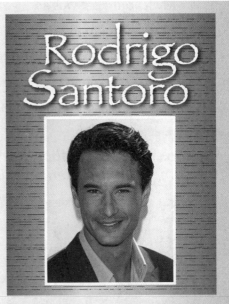

Rodrigo Santoro was born in 1975 in Petrópolis, near Rio de Janeiro, Brazil. As a child, he used to organize puppet performances during family vacations. When he was studying communications in college, he started acting in television soap operas, such as *Olho no Olho* in 1993 and *Hilda Furacão* in 1998.

After his success in soap operas, Santoro started acting in Brazilian films. His first big role was in *Bicho de Sete Cabeças* in 2001. The movie is about a young man who is wrongly kept in a mental hospital. For this role, he won the Best Actor Award at the Cartagena Film Festival. This success led to Hollywood. In 2003, Santoro acted in three movies: *Charlie's Angels: Full Throttle*, with Drew Barrymore; *The Roman Spring of Mrs. Stone*, with Helen Mirren; and *Love Actually*, with Hugh Grant. His performance as King Xerxes of Persia in the movie *300* was nominated as Best Villain at the MTV Movie Awards in 2007.

During this time, Santoro continued working in Brazil. In 2003, he starred in *Carandiru*, a film about a prison in São Paulo. He was nominated as Best Actor at the Prêmio Contigo Cinema for his performance in the 2007 film *Não Por Acaso*. More recently, he performed the role of President Raúl Castro of Cuba in *Che: Part Two* (2008) and that of Oriol in *There Be Dragons* (2011).

With this heavy workload, Santoro balances his life in Rio de Janeiro by reading, listening to music, and meditating. He also loves sports. In 2008, he played soccer with such international stars as Luís Figo and Alan Shearer for Soccer Aid, a charity that raises money for the United Nations Children's Fund (UNICEF). ■

B Check (✓) True or False. For statements that are false, write the correct information.

	True	False
1. Rodrigo Santoro studied acting in college.	☐	☐
2. He won an award for his role in *Bicho de Sete Cabeças*.	☐	☐
3. He worked in Brazil before he worked in Hollywood.	☐	☐
4. He won an MTV Movie Award for the role of King Xerxes.	☐	☐
5. He always plays very similar roles.	☐	☐
6. He once played soccer for a children's charity.	☐	☐

5 **Choose the correct word or phrase.**

1. I used to collect ___comic books___ (hobbies / scrapbooks / comic books) when I was a kid.

2. My favorite pet was a _____ (cat / beach / crayon) called Felix.

3. We used to go to _____ (video games / summer camp / toys) during our vacations. It was really fun.

4. There was a great _____ (fish / playground / soccer) in our neighborhood. We used to go there every afternoon.

6 **Look at these childhood pictures of Kate and her brother Peter. Complete the sentences using used to.**

1. In the summer, Kate and Peter sometimes
   ___used to go to summer camp.___

2. They also _____ .
   Their dog Bruno always used to follow them.

3. Kate _____
   every weekend during summer vacation. She hardly ever goes now.

4. Peter _____ .
   They're now worth a lot of money.

5. They _____ .
   They don't have any pets now.

7 *Look at the answers. Write the questions using* used to.

1. A: <u>What did you use to do in the summer?</u>

   B: We used to go to the beach.

2. A: _____

   B: No, we didn't collect shells. We used to build sand castles.

3. A: _____

   B: Yes, we did. We used to swim for hours. Then we played all

   kinds of sports.

4. A: Really? What _____

   B: Well, we used to play beach volleyball with some other kids.

5. A: _____

   B: No, we didn't. We used to win!

8 *How have you changed in the last five years? Write answers to these questions.*

1. What hobbies did you use to have five years ago? What hobbies do you

   have now?

   <u>I used to . . .</u>

   <u>Now, . . .</u>

2. What kind of music did you use to like then? What kind of music do

   you like now?

   _____

   _____

3. What kinds of clothes did you use to like to wear? What kinds of clothes

   do you like to wear now?

   _____

   _____

9 *Complete the sentences. Use the past tense of the verbs given.*

Maria: I'm an immigrant here.

I ____was____ (be) born in Chile

and _____ (grow up) there.

I _____ (come) here in 2005.

I _____ (not be) very happy at

first. Things _____ (be) difficult

for me. I _____ (not speak)

English, so I _____ (go) to a

community college and _____ (study)

English there. My English _____ (get)

better, and I _____ (find)

this job. What about you?

10 *Choose the correct responses.*

1. A: Are you from Toronto?

   B: <u>No, I'm originally from Morocco.</u>

   • No, I'm originally from Morocco.
   • Neither am I.

2. A: Tell me a little about yourself.

   B: _____

   • Sure. Nice to meet you.
   • What do you want to know?

3. A: How old were you when you moved here?

   B: _____

   • About 16.
   • About 16 years ago.

4. A: Did you learn English here?

   B: _____

   • Yes, I was 10 years old.
   • No, I studied it in Morocco.

5. A: By the way, I'm Lisa.

   B: _____

   • What's your name?
   • Glad to meet you.

2 Caught in the rush

1 *Choose the correct compound noun for each picture.*

- ☐ bicycle lane
- ☐ bus stop
- ☐ newsstand
- ☑ streetlights
- ☐ taxi stand
- ☐ traffic jam

1. streetlights

2. _____

3. _____

4. _____

5. _____

6. _____

7

Problems, problems

A Choose a solution for each problem.

Problems
1. no more parking spaces: <u>build a public parking garage</u>
2. dark streets: _____
3. no places to take children: _____
4. crime: _____
5. car accidents: _____
6. traffic jams: _____

Solutions
☐ install modern streetlights
☐ build a subway system
☐ install more traffic lights
☐ hire more police officers
☐ build more parks
☑ build a public parking garage

B Look at these solutions. Write sentences explaining the problems.
Use *too much, too many,* or *not enough* and the problems in part A.

1. <u>There aren't enough parking spaces.</u>

   The city should build a public parking garage.

2. _____

   The city should install more traffic lights.

3. _____

   The city should build a subway system.

4. _____

   The city should hire more police officers.

5. _____

   The city should build more parks.

6. _____

   The city should install modern streetlights.

C Find another way to say the problems in part B. Begin each
sentence with *There should be more/less/fewer . . . .*

1. <u>There should be more parking spaces.</u>
2. _____
3. _____
4. _____
5. _____
6. _____

3 City blues

A Match the words in columns A and B. Write the compound nouns.

A	B	
☑ air	☐ district	1. _air pollution_
☐ business	☐ garages	2. _____
☐ commuter	☐ hour	3. _____
☐ parking	☐ lines	4. _____
☐ police	☐ officers	5. _____
☐ public	☑ pollution	6. _____
☐ rush	☐ transportation	7. _____

B Complete this online post using the compound nouns in part A.

HOME HEADLINES LOCAL NEWS INTERNATIONAL BUSINESS SPORTS CONTACT US

City Forum ▶

Life in this city needs to be improved. For one thing, there are too many cars, and there is too much bad air, especially during ____rush hour____ . The _____ is terrible. This problem is particularly bad downtown in the _____ . Too many people drive their cars to work.

I think there should be more _____ at busy intersections. They could stop traffic jams. We also need fewer _____ downtown. The city spends too much money building them. It's so easy to park that too many people drive to work. However, the city doesn't spend enough money on _____ . There aren't enough _____ to the suburbs.

C Write two paragraphs about a problem in a city you know. First describe the problem and then suggest solutions.

_____

_____

_____

_____

_____

_____

_____

_____

A Read about transportation in Hong Kong. Match the photos to the descriptions in the article.

cable railway

ferry

subway

tram

Getting Around Hong Kong

Hong Kong has an excellent transportation system. If you fly there, you will arrive at one of the most modern airports in the world. And during your visit, there are many ways to get around Hong Kong.

1 _____

These have run in the streets of Hong Kong Island since 1904. They have two decks, and they carry 230,000 passengers a day. You can travel on six routes, totaling 30 kilometers (about 19 miles). You can also hire one for a private party with up to 25 guests – a great way to enjoy Hong Kong!

2 _____

Take one of these to cross from Hong Kong Island to Kowloon or to visit one of the other islands. You can also use them to travel to Macau and Guangdong. They are very safe and comfortable, and one of the cheapest boat rides in the world.

3 _____

Hong Kong's underground railway is called the MTR – the Mass Transit Railway. It is the fastest way to get around. You can catch one from the airport to all the major centers in Hong Kong. The MTR carries 2.3 million passengers a day.

4 _____

This is found on Hong Kong Island. It pulls you up Victoria Peak, which is 552 meters (about 1,800 feet) above sea level, the highest mountain on the island. The system is over 120 years old. In that time, there has never been an accident. Two cars carry up to 120 passengers each.

B Complete the chart about each type of transportation. Where you cannot find the information, write *NG* (not given).

	cable railway	ferry	subway	tram
1. How old is it?				
2. How many people use it?				
3. How safe is it?				
4. Where can you go?				

5 Complete these conversations. Use the words in the box.

> ☐ ATM   ☑ duty-free shop   ☐ sign
> ☐ bus stop   ☐ schedule

AIRPORT INFORMATION

1. A: Could you tell me where I can buy some perfume?

   B: You should try the <u>duty-free shop</u> .

2. A: Can you tell me where the buses are?

   B: Yeah, there's a _____ just

   outside this building.

3. A: Do you know where I can change money?

   B: There's a money exchange on the second floor.

   There's also an _____ over there.

4. A: Do you know what time the last train leaves

   for the city?

   B: No, but I can check the _____ .

5. A: Could you tell me where the taxi stand is?

   B: Sure. Just follow that _____ .

6 Complete the questions in this conversation at a hotel.

Guest: Could you <u>tell me where the gym is</u> ?

Clerk: Sure, the gym is on the nineteenth floor.

Guest: OK. And can you _____ ?

Clerk: Yes, the coffee shop is next to the gift shop.

Guest: The gift shop? Hmm. I need to buy something for my wife.

   Do you _____ ?

Clerk: It closes at 6:00 P.M. I'm sorry, but you'll have to wait until

   tomorrow. It's already 6:15.

Guest: OK. Oh, I'm expecting a package.

   Could you _____ ?

Clerk: Don't worry. I'll call you when it arrives.

Guest: Thanks. Just one more thing.

   Do you _____ ?

Clerk: The airport bus leaves every half hour. Anything else?

Guest: No, I don't think so. Thanks.

7 Rewrite these sentences. Find another way to say each sentence using the words given.

1. There are too many cars in this city. (fewer)
   There should be fewer cars in this city.

2. We need fewer buses and cars downtown. (traffic)
   _____

3. Where's the subway station? (Could you)
   _____

4. There isn't enough public parking. (parking garages)
   _____

5. How often does the bus come? (Do you)
   _____

6. What time does the last train leave? (Can you)
   _____

 8 Answer these questions about your city or another city you know.

The streets are closed to cars in a traffic-free zone.

1. Are there any traffic-free zones? If so, where are they located?
   _____

2. How do most people travel to and from work?
   _____

3. What's the rush hour like?
   _____

4. What's the city's biggest problem?
   _____

5. What has the city done about it?
   _____

6. Is there anything else the city could do?
   _____

Time for a change!

1 Opposites

A Write the opposites. Use the words in the box.

☐ dark   ☐ old
☐ expensive   ☐ safe
☑ inconvenient ☐ small
☐ noisy   ☐ spacious

1. convenient / _inconvenient_   5. bright / _____
2. cramped / _____   6. modern / _____
3. dangerous / _____   7. quiet / _____
4. big / _____   8. cheap / _____

B Rewrite these sentences. Find another way to say each sentence using *not . . . enough* or *too* and the words in part A.

1. The house is too expensive.
   The house isn't cheap enough.

2. The rooms aren't bright enough.
   _____

3. The living room isn't spacious enough for the family.
   _____

4. The bathroom is too old.
   _____

5. The yard isn't big enough for our pets.
   _____

6. The street is too noisy for us.
   _____

7. The neighborhood is too dangerous.
   _____

8. The location isn't convenient enough.
   _____

2 *Add the word* enough *to these sentences.*

Grammar note: enough

Enough *comes* <u>after</u> *adjectives but* <u>before</u> *nouns.*

adjective + enough

It isn't *spacious enough.*
The rooms aren't *light enough.*

enough + noun

There isn't *enough space.*
It doesn't have *enough light.*

1. The apartment isn't comfortable. ^enough

2. There aren't bedrooms.

3. It's not modern.

4. There aren't parking spaces.

5. The neighborhood doesn't have streetlights.

6. There aren't closets.

7. It's not private.

8. The living room isn't spacious.

3 *Complete this conversation. Use the words given and the comparisons in the box. (Some of the comparisons in the box can be used more than once.)*

almost as . . . as	just as many . . . as
as many . . . as	not as . . . as

Realtor: How did you like the house on Twelfth Street?

Client: Well, it's ___not as convenient as___ the apartment
on Main Street. (convenient)

Realtor: That's true, the house is less convenient.

Client: And the apartment doesn't have

_____ the house. (rooms)

Realtor: Yes, the house is more spacious.

Client: But I think there are _____

in the apartment. (closets)

Realtor: You're right. The closet space is the same.

Client: The wallpaper in the apartment is _____

_____ the wallpaper in the house. (shabby)

Realtor: I know, but you could change the wallpaper in the house.

Client: Hmm, the rent on the apartment is _____

_____ the rent on the house, but the

house is much bigger. (expensive) Oh, I can't decide.

Can you show me something else?

Home, sweet home

A Complete this questionnaire about where you live, and find your score below.

How does your home measure up?

The outside	Yes	No	To score:
1. Are you close enough to shopping?	☐	☐	How many "Yes" answers do you have?
2. Is there enough public transportation nearby?	☐	☐	
3. Are the sidewalks clean?	☐	☐	**16–20**
4. Are there good restaurants in the neighborhood?	☐	☐	It sounds like a dream home!
5. Is there a park nearby?	☐	☐	
6. Is the neighborhood quiet?	☐	☐	**11–15**
7. Is the neighborhood safe?	☐	☐	Great! All you need now is a swimming pool!
8. Is there enough parking nearby?	☐	☐	
9. Does the outside of your home look good?	☐	☐	
			6–10
The inside			Well, at least guests won't want to stay too long!
10. Are there enough bedrooms?	☐	☐	
11. Is there enough closet space?	☐	☐	
12. Is the bathroom modern?	☐	☐	**0–5**
13. Is there a washing machine?	☐	☐	Time to look for a better place to live!
14. Is there enough space in the kitchen?	☐	☐	
15. Do the stove and refrigerator work well?	☐	☐	
16. Is the living room comfortable enough?	☐	☐	
17. Is the dining area big enough?	☐	☐	
18. Are the walls newly painted?	☐	☐	
19. Are the rooms bright enough?	☐	☐	
20. Is the building warm enough in cold weather?	☐	☐	

B Write two short paragraphs about where you live. In the first paragraph describe your neighborhood, and in the second paragraph describe your home. Use the information in part A or your own information.

_____

_____

_____

_____

_____

_____

_____

_____

5 ▪ *Wishes*

A Which words or phrases often go with which verbs? Complete the chart.

- ☐ Italian
- ☐ more free time
- ☐ happier
- ☑ healthy
- ☐ my own room
- ☐ somewhere else
- ☐ karate
- ☐ to a new place

be	know	have	move
healthy			

B Describe what these people would like to change. Use *I wish* and words or phrases in part A.

1. I wish I were healthy.

2. _____

3. _____

4. _____

5. _____

6. _____

Choose the correct responses.

1. A: I wish I had an easier life.

   B: <u>Why?</u>

   - • Why?
   - • I don't like my job, either.

2. A: I wish I could retire.

   B: _____

   - • I don't like it anymore.
   - • I know what you mean.

3. A: Where do you want to move?

   B: _____

   - • Somewhere else.
   - • Something else.

4. A: I wish I could find a bigger apartment.

   B: _____

   - • Is it too large?
   - • It's very nice, though.

I wish I had an easier life!

7 **Rewrite these sentences. Find another way to say each sentence using the words given.**

1. There should be more bedrooms in my apartment. (enough)

   <u>There aren't enough bedrooms in my apartment.</u>

2. This neighborhood is safe enough. (dangerous)

   _____

3. My apartment doesn't have enough privacy. (private)

   _____

4. Our house has the same number of bedrooms as yours. (just as many)

   _____

5. I don't have enough closet space. (wish)

   _____

6. We wish we could move to a new place. (somewhere else)

   _____

7. That apartment is too small. (big)

   _____

8. I wish housework were easy. (not difficult)

   _____

A Scan the article about making wishes. Which three countries does it refer to?

Making *Wishes*

All over the world, people have always wished for things, such as peace, love, good health, and money. Over hundreds of years, people in different countries have found different ways to make wishes. Here are some interesting examples.

The Trevi Fountain in Rome, Italy, is a place where many people go to make a wish. The water from the fountain flows into a large pool of water below. To make a wish, visitors stand facing away from the fountain. Then, they use their right hand to throw a coin into the pool over their left shoulder. They believe this will bring them luck and bring them back to Rome one day. The coins in the fountain, several thousand euros each day, are given to poor people.

A very different way of making wishes happens in Anhui province in eastern China. Huangshan (which means "Yellow Mountain") is famous for its beautiful sunrises and sunsets. That's why people think it is a very romantic place. Couples go there to make a wish that they will stay together forever. Each couple buys a "love lock," or padlock, with a key. Next, they lock their padlock to a chain at the top of the mountain. Then they throw the key down the mountain so that their lock can never be opened.

In Turkey and some neighboring countries, May 5 is a special day for making wishes. People believe that each year on that day two wise men return to earth. They come to help people and give them good health. In the evening, there are street food markets selling different kinds of seasonal food and musicians playing traditional music. People write their wishes on pieces of paper and then attach the paper to a tree. Nowadays, however, some people go online and send their wishes to special websites.

B Read the article. Check (✓) the statements that are true for each place.

	Rome	Huangshan	Turkey
1. People make wishes only once a year.	☐	☐	☐
2. You need a lock and key.	☐	☐	☐
3. You put your wish on a tree.	☐	☐	☐
4. You need a coin to make your wish.	☐	☐	☐
5. Wish-making is only for couples.	☐	☐	☐
6. The money from the wishes goes to poor people.	☐	☐	☐
7. Some people make their wishes on the Internet.	☐	☐	☐

I've never heard of that!

Complete the conversation with the correct tense.

Isabel: I went to Sunrise Beach last week.

<u>Have you ever been</u>
(Did you ever go / Have you ever been)

to Sunrise Beach, Andy?

Andy: Yes, _____ . It's beautiful.
(I did / I have)

_____ there on
(Did you go / Have you gone)

the weekend?

Isabel: Yeah, I _____ .
(did / have)

I _____ on Sunday.
(went / have gone)

_____ at 4:00 A.M.
(I got up / I've gotten up)

Andy: Wow! _____ that early!
(I never woke up / I've never woken up)

Isabel: Oh, it wasn't so bad. I _____
(got / have gotten)

to the beach early to see the sun come up.

_____ a sunrise on a beach, Andy?
(Did you ever see / Have you ever seen)

Andy: No, _____ .
(I didn't / I haven't)

Isabel: Then I _____ swimming
(went / have gone)

around 6:00, but there were some strange dark shadows

in the water. _____ of sharks at Sunrise Beach?
(Did you ever hear / Have you ever heard)

Andy: Yes, _____ . I _____ a news report about sharks last summer.
(I did / I have)   (heard / have heard)

Isabel: Gee! Maybe I _____ a lucky escape on Sunday morning! Why don't you
(had / have had)

come with me next time?

Andy: Are you kidding?

2 Have you ever...?

A Look at this list and check (✓) five things you have done. Add other activities if necessary.

- ☐ go horseback riding
- ☐ cook for over 10 people
- ☐ eat raw fish
- ☐ go to a classical concert
- ☐ have green tea ice cream
- ☐ read a novel in English
- ☐ ride a motorcycle
- ☐ take a cruise
- ☐ travel abroad
- ☐ try Indian food
- ☐ _____
- ☐ _____
- ☐ _____
- ☐ _____

B Write questions about the things you checked in part A. Use *Have you ever...?*

1. Have you ever had green tea ice cream?

2. _____

3. _____

4. _____

5. _____

C Answer the questions you wrote in part B. Then use the past tense to give more information.

1. Yes, I have. I had some in a Japanese restaurant. It was delicious!

2. _____

3. _____

4. _____

5. _____

A Scan the article. What kinds of food can cause allergies?

FOOD ALLERGIES

Luis always had headaches and stomachaches. First, Luis's doctor gave him some medicine, but it didn't work. Then his doctor asked him about his favorite foods. Luis said he loved cake and ice cream. His doctor said, "Stop eating sweets." Luis stopped, but he still got headaches and stomachaches. Next, his doctor asked more questions about his diet. Luis said he ate a lot of fish. His doctor said to stop eating fish. When Luis stopped eating fish, he felt much better.

Sharon often had a very sore mouth after eating. First, she stopped drinking milk and eating cheese, but this made no difference. Then, in the summer, the problem became really bad, and it was difficult for Sharon to eat. Her doctor asked about her diet. She said she had a tomato garden, and she ate about 10 tomatoes a day. Sharon's doctor told her not to eat tomatoes. When she stopped eating tomatoes, Sharon's mouth got better.

Fred is a mechanic, but he was not able to hold his tools. His hands were swollen. First, he went to his doctor, and she gave him some medicine. The medicine didn't work. He still couldn't hold his tools. After that, his doctor asked him about his diet. Fred told her he ate a lot of bread. She told him not to eat bread or pasta. After 10 days, Fred could hold his tools again.

B Read the article. What problem did each person have? Complete the first column of the chart.

	Problem	What didn't work	What worked
Luis			
Sharon			
Fred			

C Read the article again. What didn't work? What *did work*?
Complete the rest of the chart.

4 *Eggs, anyone?*

A Here's a recipe for a mushroom omelet. Look at the pictures and number the sentences from 1 to 5.

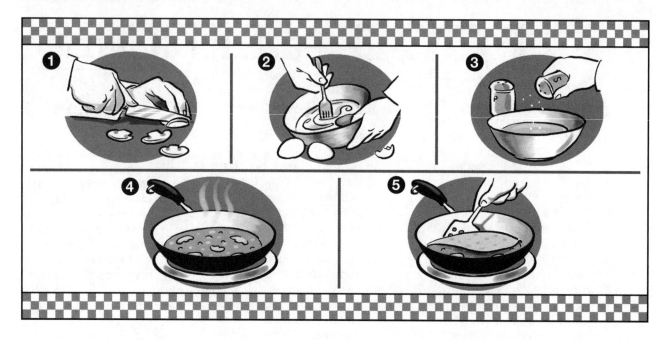

_____ After that, pour the eggs into a frying pan. Add the mushrooms and cook.

_____ Then beat the eggs in a bowl.

__1__ First, slice the mushrooms.

_____ Next, add salt and pepper to the egg mixture.

_____ Finally, fold the omelet in half. Your omelet is ready. Enjoy!

B Describe your favorite way to cook eggs. Use sequence adverbs.

How to cook: _____

5 Complete the conversation. Use the past tense or the present perfect of the verbs given.

Sylvia: I _____went_____ (go) to a Thai restaurant last night.

Jason: Really? I _____ (never eat) Thai food.

Sylvia: Oh, you should try it. It's delicious!

Jason: What _____ you _____ (order)?

Sylvia: First, I _____ (have) soup with green curry and
rice. Then I _____ (try) pad thai. It's noodles,
shrimp, and vegetables in a spicy sauce.

Jason: I _____ (not taste) pad thai before. _____ (be)
it very hot?

Sylvia: No. It _____ (be) just spicy enough. And after
that, I _____ (eat) bananas in coconut milk
for dessert.

Jason: Mmm! That sounds good.

Sylvia: It was.

6 Choose the correct word.

1. We had delicious guacamole dip and chips on Saturday night while we watched TV.
It was a great _____snack_____ (dinner / snack / meal).

2. I had a huge lunch, so I _____ (ordered / skipped / tried) dinner.

3. What _____ (appetizers / ingredients / skewers) do
you need to cook crispy fried noodles?

4. First, fry the beef in oil and curry powder and then _____
(pour / mix / toast) the coconut milk over the beef.

5. We need to leave the restaurant now. Could we have the
_____ (check / recipe / menu), please?

7 Choose the correct responses.

☐ Yuck! That sounds awful.   ☐ That sounds strange.   ☐ Mmm! That sounds good.

1. A: Have you ever tried barbecued chicken? You marinate the meat
   in barbecue sauce for about an hour and then cook it on the grill.

   B: _____

2. A: Here's a recipe called Baked Eggplant Delight. I usually bake eggplant for
   an hour, but this says you bake it for only five minutes!

   B: _____

3. A: Look at this dish – frogs' legs with bananas! I've never seen that before.

   B: _____

8 Crossword puzzle: Verbs

Use the simple past or present perfect of these verbs to complete the crossword puzzle.

☑ be   ☐ bring   ☐ decide   ☐ drive   ☐ forget   ☐ have   ☐ ride   ☐ take
☐ break ☐ buy   ☐ do   ☐ eat   ☐ give   ☐ make   ☐ skip   ☐ try

Across

1 We have never _____ to a
   Chinese restaurant.

3 I _____ all the ingredients with me.

7 _____ you eat a huge dinner last night?

8 We _____ my mother to the new
   Chilean restaurant.

11 I haven't _____ a birthday gift to my
   father yet.

12 Have you ever _____ a horse? It's great!

13 I have never _____ snails. What are
   they like?

14 Have you _____ what kind of pizza
   you would like?

Down

1 I _____ this chicken for $5.

2 Oh, I'm sorry. I just _____ a glass.

4 Victor _____ Chinese chicken for dinner.

5 I wasn't hungry this morning, so I _____ breakfast.

6 Oh, no! I _____ to buy rice.

7 Have you ever _____ a sports car?

9 I _____ Greek food for the first time last night.

10 Have you ever _____ Peruvian ceviche?
   It's delicious.

5 Going places

1 Vacation plans

A Which words or phrases often go with which verbs?
Complete the chart. Use each word or phrase only once.

☐ a camper	☐ lots of hiking	☐ sailing lessons
☐ camping	☐ my email	☐ some fishing
☐ a car	☐ my reading	☐ something exciting
☐ a condominium	☐ my studying	☐ swimming
☑ long walks	☐ on vacation	☐ a vacation

take	do	go
long walks		

rent	catch up on

B Write four things you plan to do on your next vacation. Use *be going to* and
the information in part A or your own information.

Vacation plans

1. _____
2. _____
3. _____
4. _____

C Write four sentences about your possible vacation plans. Use *will* with *maybe*,
probably, *I guess*, or *I think*. Use the information in part A or your own information.

Possible plans

1. _____
2. _____
3. _____
4. _____

2 *Complete the conversation. Use* be going to *or* will *and the information on the notepads.*

Dave: So, Stella, do you have any vacation plans?

Stella: Well, _I'm going to paint my apartment_ because the walls are a really ugly color. What about you?

Dave: _____ and take a long drive.

Stella: Where are you going to go?

Dave: I'm not sure. _____ . I haven't seen her in a long time.

Stella: That sounds nice. I like to visit my family, too.

Dave: Yes, and _____ for a few days. I haven't been hiking in months. How about you? Are you going to do anything else on your vacation?

Stella: _____ . I have a lot of work to do before school starts.

Dave: That doesn't sound like much fun.

Stella: Oh, I am planning to have some fun, too. _____ . I love to swim in the ocean!

Stella's Pad

paint my apartment - yes

catch up on my studying - probably

relax on the beach - yes

DAVE'S PAD

rent a car - yes

visit my sister Joanne - probably

go to the mountains - maybe

3 *Travel plans*

A Look at these answers. Write questions using *be going to*.

1. A: _Where are you going to go?_

   B: I'm going to go someplace nice and quiet.

2. A: _____

   B: I'm going to drive.

3. A: _____

   B: I'm going to stay in a condominium. My friend has one near the beach.

4. A: _____

   B: No, I'm going to travel by myself.

B Use the cues to write other answers to the questions in part A. Use *be going to* or *will*.

1. _I'm not going to go to a busy place._ (not go / busy place)

2. _____ (maybe / take the train)

3. _____ (not stay / hotel)

4. _____ (I think / ask a friend)

4 Travel ads

A Scan the travel ad. Where can tourists see beautiful nature scenes?

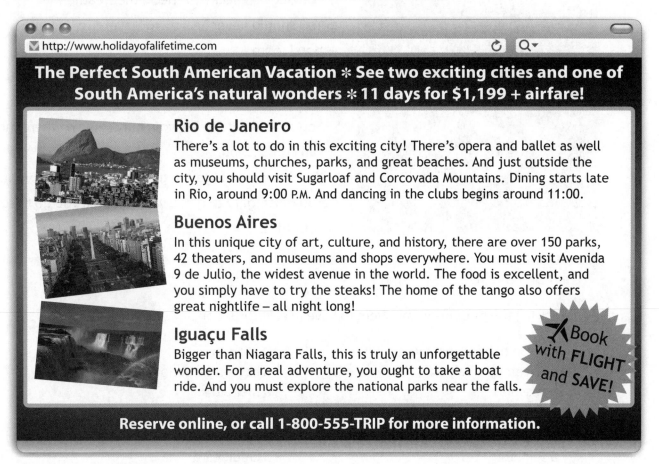

http://www.holidayofalifetime.com

The Perfect South American Vacation ✳ **See two exciting cities and one of South America's natural wonders** ✳ **11 days for $1,199 + airfare!**

Rio de Janeiro

There's a lot to do in this exciting city! There's opera and ballet as well as museums, churches, parks, and great beaches. And just outside the city, you should visit Sugarloaf and Corcovada Mountains. Dining starts late in Rio, around 9:00 P.M. And dancing in the clubs begins around 11:00.

Buenos Aires

In this unique city of art, culture, and history, there are over 150 parks, 42 theaters, and museums and shops everywhere. You must visit Avenida 9 de Julio, the widest avenue in the world. The food is excellent, and you simply have to try the steaks! The home of the tango also offers great nightlife – all night long!

Iguaçu Falls

Bigger than Niagara Falls, this is truly an unforgettable wonder. For a real adventure, you ought to take a boat ride. And you must explore the national parks near the falls.

✈ Book with FLIGHT and SAVE!

Reserve online, or call 1-800-555-TRIP for more information.

B Read the ad. Check (✓) True or False. For the statements that are false, write the correct information.

	True	False
1. People have dinner late in Rio de Janeiro.	☐	☐
2. Buenos Aires has the longest avenue in the world.	☐	☐
3. Niagara Falls is bigger than Iguaçu Falls.	☐	☐
4. Both Rio de Janeiro and Buenos Aires have exciting nightlife.	☐	☐
5. Rio de Janeiro, Buenos Aires, and Iguaçu Falls have unforgettable parks and beaches.	☐	☐

5 *Circle the correct word or words to give advice to travelers.*

1. You ought (check / (to check)) the weather.
2. You should never (leave / to leave) cash in your hotel room.
3. You need (take / to take) your credit card with you.
4. You have (pay / to pay) an airport tax.
5. You should (let / to let) your family know where they can contact you.
6. You'd better not (go / to go) out alone late at night.
7. You must (get / to get) a vaccination if you go to some countries.

6 *Take it or leave it?*

A Check (✓) the most important item to have in each situation.

1. A vacation to a foreign country
   - ☐ an overnight bag
   - ☑ a passport
   - ☐ a driver's license

2. A mountain-climbing vacation
   - ☐ a suitcase
   - ☐ a visa
   - ☐ hiking boots

3. A sailing trip
   - ☐ a hotel reservation
   - ☐ a first-aid kit
   - ☐ an ATM card

4. A visit to a temple
   - ☐ a credit card
   - ☐ suitable clothes
   - ☐ a plane ticket

B Give advice to these people. Use the words or phrases in the box and the items in part A. Use each word or phrase only once.

| ☐ ought to | ☐ need to | ☐ should | ☑ had better ('d better) |

1. Yuko is going on a vacation to a foreign country.

   She'd better take a passport.

2. Michelle and Steven are going on a mountain-climbing vacation.

   _____

3. Philip and Julia are planning a sailing trip.

   _____

4. Jack is going to visit a temple.

   _____

You don't need to take that!

Your friends are planning to drive across North America and camp along the way. What advice can you give them? Write eight sentences using the expressions in the box and some of the cues below.

You don't have to . . .	You ought to . . .
You have to . . .	You should . . .
You must . . .	You shouldn't . . .
You need to . . .	You'd better . . .

bring cooking equipment
buy good quality camping equipment
buy maps and travel guides
forget a first-aid kit
forget your passport or identification
get a GPS device for your car

pack a lot of luggage
remember to bring insect spray
remember to bring a jacket
take a credit card
take a lot of cash
take your driver's license

1. *You have to bring cooking equipment.*
2. _____
3. _____
4. _____
5. _____
6. _____
7. _____
8. _____

8 *Rewrite these sentences. Find another way to say each sentence using the words given.*

1. I'm not going to go on vacation on my own. (alone)

_____

2. I don't want to travel with anyone. (by myself)

_____

3. You ought to travel with a friend. (should)

_____

4. It's necessary to get a vaccination. (must)

_____

A Read these notes, and then write a description of your vacation. Use *be going to* for the plans you've decided on. Use *will* with *maybe, probably, I guess,* or *I think* for the plans you're not sure about.

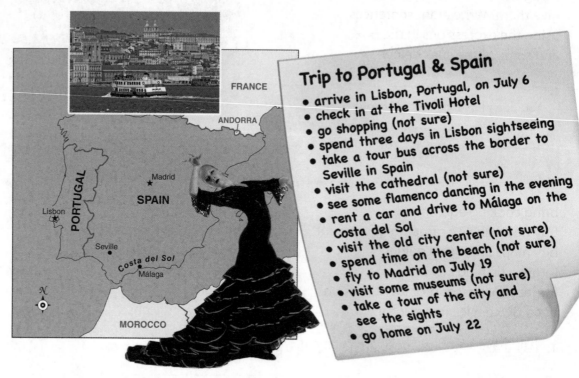

Trip to Portugal & Spain
- arrive in Lisbon, Portugal, on July 6
- check in at the Tivoli Hotel
- go shopping (not sure)
- spend three days in Lisbon sightseeing
- take a tour bus across the border to Seville in Spain
- visit the cathedral (not sure)
- see some flamenco dancing in the evening
- rent a car and drive to Málaga on the Costa del Sol
- visit the old city center (not sure)
- spend time on the beach (not sure)
- fly to Madrid on July 19
- visit some museums (not sure)
- take a tour of the city and see the sights
- go home on July 22

I'm going to arrive in Lisbon, Portugal, on July 6 and check in at the
Tivoli Hotel. Then maybe I'll go shopping. . . .

_____

_____

_____

_____

_____

_____

_____

_____

B Write five things you need to remember before you go on vacation.

1. I have to print my boarding pass.

2. _____

3. _____

4. _____

5. _____

6 OK. No problem!

1 Write responses to these requests. Use *it* or *them*.

1. Please take out the trash.

   OK, I'll take it out.

2. Please put the dishes away.

   _____

3. Hang up the towels.

   _____

4. Turn off the lights, please.

   _____

5. Turn on the radio.

   _____

2 Two-part verbs

A Use the words in the box to make two-part verbs. (You may use words more than once.)

| away | down | off | on | out | up |

1. clean ___up___   6. take _____

2. hang _____   7. take _____

3. let _____   8. throw _____

4. pick _____   9. turn _____

5. put _____   10. turn _____

B Make requests with the two-part verbs in part A. Then give a reason for making the request.

1. Please clean up your room. It's dirty.

2. _____

3. _____

4. _____

5. _____

3 ▸ Choose the correct word.

1. Hang up your _____coat_____ . (books / coat / trash)

2. Take out the _____ . (groceries / trash / yard)

3. Turn down the _____ . (garbage / TV / toys)

4. Pick up your _____ . (lights / things / yard)

5. Put away your _____ . (clothes / microwave / dog)

6. Turn on the _____ . (magazines / mess / radio)

4 ▸ What's your excuse?

A Complete these requests. Use the sentences in the box.

☐ It's a mess.   ☑ They shouldn't be on the floor.
☐ It's too loud.   ☐ The milk is getting warm.
☐ They're dirty.

1. Pick up your clothes, please. _They shouldn't be on the floor._

2. Please put the groceries away. _____

3. Take your shoes off. _____

4. Clean up the kitchen, please. _____

5. Turn down the music. _____

B Write an excuse for each request in part A.

1. _Sorry, but there isn't enough room in my closet._

2. _____

3. _____

4. _____

5. _____

5 *Chores, chores, chores*

A Scan the article. What are some ways to get children to do chores?

Helping out at home

In many families, household chores can be a problem. Who does them? Who should do them? In the past, many women stayed at home and did all the chores. Husbands went out to work and expected their wives to clean and cook. Nowadays, though, more and more women have jobs outside the home. So most people think that both wives and husbands should share responsibility for doing household chores. But what about kids? Should children help their parents around the house? If so, how old should they be when they start? How often should they help? And should they get money for helping?

Many people agree that children should help around the house. Doing chores is one way that children can learn to take responsibility for the mess they make. Some even say that young children should help in the home. They can do easy jobs – a child of six or seven years old, for example, can help do the laundry by separating dark-colored and light-colored clothes.

One problem is making sure that children and teenagers help regularly with chores. To solve this problem, some people suggest making a list of household chores, either on paper or on a computer spreadsheet. The list can have four parts: daily chores (such as doing the dishes), weekly chores (washing the car), monthly chores (cleaning the refrigerator), and yearly chores (cleaning the garage). Another suggestion to make sure that children do jobs around the house is to pay them. Some people say that this helps children and teenagers learn how to manage money, but others think it's wrong to pay kids to help because they are part of the family. After all, no one pays Mom or Dad to do the chores!

B Read the article. Then answer these questions.

1. Why do some people think that both wives and husbands should do household chores?

   _____

2. Why do many people think that children should do some chores?

   _____

3. What kinds of chores can young children do?

   _____

4. What reasons are given for and against paying young people to do chores?

   _____

   _____

   _____

6 *Rewrite these sentences. Find another way to say each sentence using the words given.*

1. Turn off your cell phone, please. (Can)

   Can you turn off your cell phone, please?

2. Take this form to the office. (Would you mind)

   _____

3. Please turn the TV down. (Could)

   _____

4. Don't leave wet towels on the floor. (Would you mind)

   _____

5. Text me today's homework assignment. (Would)

   _____

6. Pass me that book, please. (Can)

   _____

7 *Choose the correct responses.*

1. A: Could you lend me some money?

   B: _Sure._____

   - Sure.
   - Oh, sorry.
   - No, thanks.

2. A: Would you mind helping me?

   B: _____

   - Sorry, I can't right now.
   - No, thanks.
   - I forgot.

3. A: Excuse me, but you're sitting in my seat.

   B: _____

   - I'll close it.
   - Not right now.
   - Oh, I'm sorry. I didn't realize that.

4. A: Would you like to come in?

   B: _____

   - That's no excuse.
   - Sorry, I forgot.
   - All right. Thanks.

5. A: Would you mind not leaving your dirty

   clothes on the floor?

   B: _____

   - OK, thanks.
   - Oh, all right. I'll put them away.
   - Excuse me. I'll pay for them.

6. A: Can you hand me the remote control?

   B: _____

   - No problem.
   - You could, too.
   - I'll make sure.

8 **For each complaint, apologize and either give an excuse, admit a mistake, make an offer, or make a promise.**

1. Customer: This steak is very tough. I can't eat it.

   Waiter: _Oh, I'm sorry. I'll get you another one._

2. Steven: You're late! I've been here for half an hour!

   Katie: _____

3. Roommate 1: Could you turn the TV down?
   I'm trying to study, and the noise is bothering me.

   Roommate 2: _____

4. Father: You didn't take out the garbage this morning.

   Son: _____

5. Customer: I brought this laptop in last week,
   but it's still not working right.

   Salesperson: _____

6. Neighbor 1: Could you do something about your dog?
   It barks all night and keeps me awake.

   Neighbor 2: _____

7. Resident: Would you mind moving your car?
   You're parked in my parking space.

   Visitor: _____

8. Teacher: Please put away your papers. You left them on
   your desk yesterday.

   Student: _____

9 **Choose the correct words.**

1. Throw those empty bottles away.

   Put them in the _____ (recycling bin / living room / refrigerator).

2. Would you mind picking up some _____

   (dry cleaning / groceries / towels)? We need coffee, milk, and rice.

3. Turn the _____ (faucet / oven / stereo) off. Water

   costs money!

4. My neighbor made a _____ (mistake / request / promise).

   He said, "I'll be sure to stop my dog from barking."

10 Requests

A Match the words and phrases in columns A and B.

A	B	
☑ pick up	☐ your bedroom	1. <u>pick up some milk</u>
☐ not criticize	☑ some milk	2. _____
☐ mail	☐ the groceries	3. _____
☐ not talk	☐ your sunglasses	4. _____
☐ put away	☐ these bills	5. _____
☐ take off	☐ the TV	6. _____
☐ turn down	☐ so loudly	7. _____
☐ clean up	☐ my friends	8. _____

B Write requests using the phrases in part A.

1. <u>Would you mind picking up some milk?</u>
2. _____
3. _____
4. _____
5. _____
6. _____
7. _____
8. _____

11 Write five complaints you have about a friend or a relative. Then write a wish for each complaint.

1. My roommate is always using my hair dryer.

   <u>I wish she had her own hair dryer.</u>

2. _____

   _____

3. _____

   _____

4. _____

   _____

5. _____

   _____

7 What's this for?

1 *What are these items used for? Write a sentence about each item using* **used for** *and the information in the box.*

☐ do boring jobs	☐ store and transmit data	☐ transmit radio and TV programs
☑ write reports	☐ determine your exact location	

1 computer

2 robot

3 satellite

4 flash drive

5 GPS device

1. A computer is used for writing reports.

2. _____

3. _____

4. _____

5. _____

2 *Check (✓) the technology and what it does. Then write sentences using* **be used to.**

1. ☑ text messages ☑ cell phone ☐ photocopies

   A cell phone is used to send text messages.

2. ☐ MP4 player ☐ videos ☐ voice

   _____

3. ☐ games ☐ satellites ☐ weather

   _____

4. ☐ videos ☐ messages ☐ video camera

   _____

5. ☐ the Internet ☐ robots ☐ information

   _____

3 Choose the correct word to complete each sentence.
Use the correct form of the word.

1. Robots are used to ____perform____ (find / perform / study) many dangerous jobs.

2. Computers are used to _____ (connect / download / sing) music.

3. Satellites are used for _____ (check / transmit / write) radio programs.

4. Home computers are used to _____ (play / pay / have) bills.

5. External hard drives are used for _____ (back up / email / buy) data.

6. Airport scanners are used to _____ (hide / allow / find) dangerous items.

4 Complete the sentences with **used to, is used to,** or **are used to.**

1. My sister _____used to_____ visit me on weekends when I was in college.

2. People _____ write letters, but nowadays they usually send emails instead.

3. A cell phone _____ make calls and send texts.

4. I _____ have a desktop computer, but now I just use a laptop.

5. We download all of our movies. We _____ buy DVDs, but not anymore.

6. Wi-Fi networks _____ access the Internet wirelessly.

5 Garage sales

A Scan these ads for garage sales. Which ones include electronics?

Garage Sales This Weekend
Next Week >

A **HOUSEHOLD** goods, including refrigerator, dishwasher, microwave oven, TV, stereo, couch, 2 bikes. Sat. 9–3. 1528 Williams Dr. Remember to bring cash only!

B **MOVING!** Office supplies, books, shelves, desk and office chair, and lots of old CDs! Sat. 8–3. 32 Harbor Rd.

C **VALUABLE** Mexican paintings, antique chairs, oriental rugs, collection of old Japanese kimonos and other clothes from around the world, old maps, gold coins. Sun. 11–5. 2039 E. 8th St. Try to arrive early!

D **COLLECTOR GOES BROKE!** Everything must go! Collection of shells, stamps, and coins from around the world, old postcards, photos. Sun. noon to 7. 9734 Date St. Make sure to tell your friends.

E **ELECTRICAL** engineer retiring. Laptop computers, cable modems, laser printers, fax machine, software for word processing and creating budgets, even a few video games. 9–5 Sat. & Sun. 2561 Canada Dr.

B Read the ads. Which garage sale should these people attend? (More than one answer may be possible.)

1. _____ Linda has just started her own business. She likes to play music while she works.

2. _____ Edmund and Tina decorate homes. They always use old and unusual items to make the houses they decorate more interesting.

3. _____ James needs some furniture for his new apartment.

4. _____ Rebecca wants to have an office in her home.

5. _____ Sam likes collecting interesting and unusual things from different countries.

6 *Useful types of websites*

A Match the types of websites with how people use them.

Types of websites	How people use websites
_e_ answer sites	a. find out what's happening in the world
_____ blogs	b. share information and photos with friends
_____ dating sites	c. find information on the Internet
_____ gaming sites	d. write and edit web pages
_____ media sharing sites	e. ask and answer questions online
_____ news sites	f. find a partner
_____ search engines	g. play online games
_____ social networking sites	h. post online diaries
_____ wiki sites	i. upload videos and music

B Do you use any of the types of websites in part A? What do you use them for? Write sentences.

1. <u>I use answer sites to ask and answer questions online.</u>   OR

   <u>I use answer sites for asking and answering questions online.</u>

2. _____

3. _____

4. _____

 Put these instructions in order. Number them from 1 to 5.

⬅ ➡   Social Networking   Search

Getting Started with Social Networking

_____ Next, check what the site has to offer you. Don't worry if you can't understand all its functions.

_____ First of all, join a social networking site. Choose a site where you already know people.

_____ After that, use the site's search features to find friends. Be sure to browse through groups who share your interests.

_____ Finally, invite people to be your friend. Try not to be shy! Lots of people may be waiting to hear from you.

_____ Then customize your profile page. For example, play with the colors to make the page reflect your personality. Now you're ready to start exploring!

8 *Write a sentence about each picture using an expression in the box.*

☐ Be sure to . . . ☑ Make sure to . . . ☐ Try not to . . .
☐ Don't forget to . . . ☐ Remember to . . . ☐ Try to . . .

 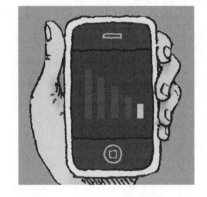 

1. Make sure to turn off your computer.

2. _____

3. _____

4. _____

5. _____

6. _____

9 *Write* **a** *or an* **an** *in the correct places. (There are nine other places in this paragraph.)*

My brother just bought ᵃ smartphone. It's really great. It has lot of high-tech features. In fact, it's amazing handheld computer, not just cell phone. For example, it has Wi-Fi connectivity, so my brother can connect to the Internet in most places. He can send message to friend by email or through social networking site. He can also find out where he is because it has GPS app. That's perfect for my brother because he likes mountain climbing. He'll never get lost again! His smartphone also has excellent camera, so he can take photos of his climbing trips. And, of course, it's phone. So he can talk to his girlfriend anytime he wants!

10 Rewrite these sentences. Find another way to say each sentence using the words given.

1. I use my computer for paying bills. (online)

   I pay my bills online.

2. It breaks very easily. (fragile)

   _____

3. Take it out of the outlet. (unplug)

   _____

4. Remember to keep it dry. (spill)

   _____

5. Don't let the battery die. (recharge)

   _____

11 Look at the pictures and complete this conversation. Choose the correct responses.

A: What a day! First, my microwave didn't work.

B: What happened?

A: *It burned my lunch.*
   - It didn't cook my lunch.
   - It burned my lunch.

   Then I tried to use my computer,

   but that didn't work either.

B: Why not?

A: _____
   - I couldn't get a Wi-Fi signal.
   - I couldn't turn it on.

   After that, I tried to use the vacuum cleaner.

B: Let me guess. It didn't pick up the dirt.

A: Worse! _____
   - It made a terrible noise.
   - It spread dirt around the room.

B: Did you have your robot help?

A: Well, I tried to get it to clean the outside

   windows. _____
   - But it refused.
   - It did a great job.

B: I don't blame it! You live on the 50th floor!

8 Let's celebrate!

1 Complete this paragraph with the words in the box.

- ☐ celebrate
- ☐ fireworks
- ☑ holidays
- ☐ picnic
- ☐ customs
- ☐ get-togethers
- ☐ music
- ☐ streamers

One of the most important national ____holidays____ in the United States is Independence Day. This is the day when Americans _____ winning their independence from Britain almost 250 years ago. There are many _____ for Independence Day. Most towns, big and small, mark this holiday with parades and _____ . They decorate with lots of _____ , usually in red, white, and blue, the colors of the U.S. flag. Bands play patriotic _____ . It's also a day when many Americans have family _____ . Families celebrate with a barbecue or a _____ .

2 Complete the sentences with the clauses in the box.

- ☐ when I feel sad and depressed
- ☐ when people have to pay their taxes
- ☐ when school starts
- ☐ when summer vacation begins

1. I hate April 15! In the United States, it's the day
_____ . I always owe the government money.

2. June is my favorite month. It's the month _____
_____ . I always head straight for the beach.

3. September is my least favorite month. It's the month
_____ . Good-bye, summer!

4. I have never liked winter. It's a season _____ .
The cold weather always affects my mood negatively.

3 Crossword puzzle: Special days

Use words from the unit to complete the crossword puzzle.

Across

4 _____ is the time of year when there are a lot of weddings in the U.S.

5 People like to play _____ on each other on April Fools' Day.

6 We always have a _____ at our house on New Year's Eve.

8 On Labor Day, people in the U.S. _____ workers.

9 Janice and Nick are getting married soon. They plan to have a small _____ with just a few family members.

11 My friends and family gave me some very nice _____ on my birthday.

14 People waited along the route for hours to see the _____ pass through the streets.

15 I gave my grandmother a bouquet of _____ on Mother's Day.

16 People in the United States and Canada celebrate the _____ at Thanksgiving.

Down

1 Everyone in my family eats _____ on Thanksgiving.

2 Hurry up with the balloons and the streamers! We need to finish the _____ before our guests arrive.

3 To celebrate the new year, many people shoot _____ into the air at night.

7 Tomorrow is my parents' twenty-fifth wedding _____ .

10 November 2 is the day when my family and I go to the cemetery to clean the _____ of our ancestors.

12 My favorite _____ are spring and summer.

13 I send my friends _____ on special occasions.

A lot to celebrate!

A Read about these special days in the United States.
Do you celebrate any of them in your country?

EVENT		DAY	HOW PEOPLE CELEBRATE IT
	Martin Luther King Jr. Day	3rd Monday in January	This is the day people honor the life and work of the civil rights leader Martin Luther King Jr.
	Presidents' Day	3rd Monday in February	This day honors two great presidents of the United States, George Washington and Abraham Lincoln.
	April Fools' Day	April 1	This is a day when people play tricks on friends. Websites sometimes post funny stories or advertise fake products.
	Earth Day	April 22	This is a day when people think about protecting the earth. People give speeches about ways to help take care of the environment.
	Mother's Day	2nd Sunday in May	People honor their mothers by giving cards and gifts and having a family gathering.
	Father's Day	2nd Sunday in June	People honor their fathers by giving them cards and presents.
	Independence Day	July 4	Americans celebrate their country's independence from Britain. There are parades and fireworks.
	Labor Day	1st Monday in September	People honor workers and celebrate the end of summer. Most people have the day off, and they have barbecues with friends and family.

B Complete the chart. Check (✓) the correct answers.

	Americans give each other gifts on:	Americans don't give gifts on:
Martin Luther King Jr. Day	☐	☐
Presidents' Day	☐	☐
April Fools' Day	☐	☐
Earth Day	☐	☐
Mother's Day	☐	☐
Father's Day	☐	☐
Independence Day	☐	☐
Labor Day	☐	☐

5 *What happens at these times in your country? Complete the sentences.*

1. Before a man and woman get married, <u>they</u>
   <u>usually date each other.</u>

2. When someone has a birthday, _____
   _____

3. Before some people eat a meal, _____
   _____

4. After a student graduates, _____
   _____

5. When a woman gets engaged, _____
   _____

6. When a couple has their first child, _____
   _____

7. When a person retires, _____
   _____

6 *Complete the paragraph with the information in the box.*
Add a comma where necessary.

> **Grammar note: Adverbial clauses of time**
>
> **The adverbial clause can come before or after the main clause.**
> **Before the main clause, add a comma.**
> When a couple gets married, they often receive gifts.
> **Do not add a comma after the main clause.**
> A couple often receives gifts when they get married.

- ☐ before the wedding reception ends
- ☐ many newlyweds have to live with relatives
- ☐ most couples like to be alone
- ☐ when they have enough money to pay for it

Newly married couples often leave on their honeymoon _____
_____ . When they go on their
honeymoon _____ .
After they come back from their honeymoon _____
_____ . They can only live in their own place
_____ .

7 Write three paragraphs about marriage customs in your country.
In the first paragraph, write about what happens before the wedding.
In the second paragraph, write about the wedding ceremony.
In the final paragraph, write about what happens after the wedding.

_____
_____
_____
_____
_____
_____
_____
_____
_____

Japan   Morocco   Scotland   India

8 Choose the correct word or phrase.

1. Wedding _____ (celebrations / flowers / birthdays) are often held in a restaurant or hotel.

2. Children's Day is a day when people in many countries _____ (court / honor / occur) their children.

3. Fall is the _____ (custom / get-together / season) when North Americans celebrate Thanksgiving.

4. In Indonesia, on Nyepi Day, Balinese people _____ (last / eat / observe) a day of silence to begin the new year.

9 Rewrite these sentences. Find another way to say each sentence using the words given.

1. Everyone in the family comes to my parents' home on Thanksgiving. (get together)

   <u>Everyone in the family gets together at my parents' home on Thanksgiving.</u>

2. Many people have parties on New Year's Eve. (New Year's Eve / when)

   _____

3. At the end of the year, Japanese people give and receive *oseibo* presents to show their appreciation for the people in their lives. (exchange)

   _____

4. June is the month when many Brazilians celebrate the Festa Junina. (in June)

   _____

5. In Sweden, people observe Midsummer's Day around June 21. (occur)

   _____

10 Imagine you are in a foreign country and someone has invited you to a New Year's Eve party. Ask questions about the party using the words in the box or your own ideas.

| ☐ clothes | ☐ midnight | ☐ sing and dance |
| ☐ fireworks | ☑ present | ☐ special food or drink |

1. <u>Should I bring a New Year's present?</u>

2. _____

3. _____

4. _____

5. _____

6. _____